MARK DANDO & DOUG RICHAI
of Coloured Square Ltd.

Since 1998, they've evolved their unique approach to learning and development via their simple but powerful Coloured Square Universal Toolkit™. They've provoked thousands of people in many big-name organisations to change the way they think and behave, in order to be more effective and get more of what they want in their work and in their lives.

They are specialists in noticing and challenging the mindsets which people are currently using – the mindsets which affect their ability to adopt new behaviours.

Mark lives in Bristol. Doug lives in Nottingham. This is their second book. They both love the work they do.

To find out more, visit the Coloured Square website at www.colouredsquare.com.

Also by Mark Dando & Doug Richardson

Squeeze Your Time

Kill the Robot

■ A Mindset Book ■

Mark Dando & Doug Richardson

SilverWood

Published in 2017 by SilverWood Books

SilverWood Books Ltd
14 Small Street, Bristol, BS1 1DE, United Kingdom
www.silverwoodbooks.co.uk

ISBN 978-1-78132-527-8 (paperback)
ISBN 978-1-78132-528-5 (ebook)

British Library Cataloguing in Publication Data
A CIP catalogue record for this book is available from
the British Library

Page design and typesetting by SilverWood Books
Printed on responsibly sourced paper

Kill the Robot

Introduction

Every day we face an onslaught of information.

Every day we are expected to absorb, remember and make sense of a deluge of ideas, concepts, plans, actions, data, requests, names, faces, facts, numbers, flow charts, pie charts and bar charts.

And in organisational life, every day so many of us are required to attend meetings, conferences, teleconferences, one-to-ones, huddles, updates, online meetings, seminars, training sessions and 'just a quick coffee' with the boss, at which this onslaught of information is presented to us, or at us.

If we're to cope with this onslaught, then
The clarity   The impact   The memorability
of the information we receive needs to be good.

But every week we see and experience so many situations where the people presenting have spent very little of their energy considering *how to present* their messages to increase this clarity, impact and memorability.

Instead, like a group of well-oiled robots running a programme that's never been declared, each presenter delivers their message in a similar (or the same) manner.

This book is intended to give you a set of provocative ideas to help you kill the robot in you, and get back to more interesting, more impactful and more memorable human presentations.

It's about clarity of thinking, developing more choices and delivering differently with confidence.

Thinking	+	Choices	=	Confidence

+ | Clarity, Impact & Memorability |

By itself, this book won't make you more confident – but if you practise the thinking disciplines it describes, over time your confidence will increase.

Take a look at this photograph:

When faced with this meeting room, what do you immediately think are the tools you're supposed to present with?

Where do you immediately think you're supposed to present?

When faced with this meeting room, many people we've worked with over the last ten years immediately think their presentation tools should look like this:

And when faced with this meeting room, many people we've worked with immediately think they're supposed to present from a very particular position.

The probability that many, many people are going to communicate using the same tools, standing in pretty much the same place as every other person presenting today, this week, this month, this year has big implications for the quality of life in organisations.

What's particularly interesting is that the presenters haven't usually been told that this is what they have to do – 'stand here, use this' – it's not an explicit rule. Somehow this thinking creeps upon them; a groupthink, an unconscious collective mindset, an undeclared robot programme that talks to them about what's expected.

Behind these assumptions about what you're supposed to do in a meeting room like the one in the pictures above are some simple mindset choices. These mindset choices are what this book is about.

If you've read one of our mindset books before then you'll know that this book will contain plenty of how-tos about presentations, but essentially, it's powered by an examination of some typical thinking patterns which we've noticed people use when preparing and delivering presentations.

It will proceed by challenging you to make some mindset choices; to consider some alternative thinking patterns which you could adopt in order to allow yourself some different approaches to presenting.

Kill the robot!

Chapter One

Mindset choices

When we work with people on delivering presentations, we notice many common mindsets or thinking patterns which seem to arise in response to the madness of organisational life.

For example, we notice that people who are used to attending meetings in which everyone is expected to 'do a presentation' can think about this task in very particular ways. Many people we've worked with are often thinking about such presentations as:

Just another job to get done   or

Another task on my list to get through

They aren't necessarily aware that they're thinking about presenting this way – that this is their mindset – it just happens over time.

As a result of thinking this way, some other *more productive thoughts don't necessarily happen*, and we notice that people who are thinking:

It's just another job to get done or

Another task on my list to get through

don't necessarily think:

What am I trying to achieve with this presentation? or

How do I want to affect the people listening? or even

Why bother to present at all? I could send an email instead.
I could leave a voice mail instead.
I could have coffee with them.

And a big problem with all of this is that often the answer to the question:

Why bother to present at all? becomes

Because I've been asked to or

Everyone else will, so I'd better

Of course, most people we work with aren't adopting only these rather passive mindsets. In answer to the question "Why bother to present at all?" they're often adopting some more productive mindsets as well – mindsets such as:

I need to look professional   I need to fit in

I need to conform   which are more productive versions of

These *are* essential choices – it's very important to be able to look professional when needed. And it's important to conform enough, otherwise you run the risk of your message being dismissed (or worse – that you are!).

But what we find is that many people adopt these particular mindsets much too early when thinking about a presentation, and then they can't get past them – they allow them to define their presentation.

We've attended the World Business Forum in New York City on three occasions; a two-day parade of fantastic speakers – presidents, CEOs, filmmakers, economists and leadership gurus. Out of the forty plus speakers we've seen, the ones we still talk about the most – the ones whose messages we still remember most clearly – definitely were *not* planning and delivering their presentations with mindsets based on:

looking professional or conforming

On the other hand, we still talk about one CEO we heard – a very big player on the world business stage – for a different reason. We still talk about her because we can't remember anything that she talked about, which is curious because her presentation was amazingly professional, slick and well-rehearsed – as was she. For us, the big issue was that whilst we couldn't say her presentation was boring, we knew we'd seen many versions of it many times before – it was very professional, but it just wasn't interesting.

Thinking back, we realise this presentation might have been put together with a mindset of:

`FYI` or `An update on what we're doing and how`

Which is fine if you know your audience is really, really interested in this, and it's what they want. And here's the key – we don't think this very powerful, very successful and important person had considered her audience for her presentation. Easily done. And because she hadn't considered her audience, she didn't really have an objective. For us, 'an update' and 'FYI' are not objectives. And as a result of these non-objectives, it seemed to us that she'd probably missed another crucial mindset:

`What impact do I want to create today?`

Take heart, presenters everywhere. If such a high-profile, successful, powerful and well-trained-in-the-art-of-presentation CEO can do such a thoroughly professional and *unimpressive* job on a particular day, then there's hope for all of us!

Now, it's possible you're already finding this challenge to notice and choose your thoughts – *Shall I choose the pink thought or the blue one?* – a little bit too much like hard work. No problem. There's still time to stop reading this book and go and find a simple 'how to deliver professional presentations' book, which won't give you a headache, and will help you join the ranks of corporate robots everywhere who enjoy attending endless meetings where nobody really learns a great deal or achieves a great deal, "but at least we're all still in a job and can invent more endless discussions with which to fill our time".

Happy being a corporate robot?
Leave here.
We're sorry to have bothered you.
We're sorry to have wasted your time.
Get this book on eBay right now!

No? Sticking around?

Great – let's get on and explore how you can kill your robot and get a more interesting and impactful version of you presenting again.

Chapter Two

What are mindsets?

If you've read one of our books before you'll have read the description below. We include it again here as a brief recap on this essential information before we get on with the business of reinventing your presentations.

Throughout this book, when we mention 'mindsets' we're thinking of a specific process your brain uses to filter for information.

Our senses take in a deluge of information every second; millions of bits of data flooding in via eyes, ears, nose etc. The brain would be overwhelmed if it actively tried to process all this information, so it doesn't. Our brains actively make decisions about what information to process and what information to filter out of our attention. As a result, the larger proportion of data received every second is discarded, or not processed, by our conscious mind.

As a consequence of this we often miss large changes to our visual field, and we can fail to notice something which is right in front of our eyes – something which would be obvious to somebody else who knows it's there, knows where to look, or knows it's about to happen.

So when we mention mindsets we're talking about this process by which you 'set' your mind to filter for information, i.e. the largely unconscious neurological process by which your brain decides what information to pay attention to and what information to filter out or discard.

As yet, it's not very clear what it is that sets your mind in this way, but it's probably a very long list of factors: your beliefs, how you were brought up, what you did yesterday, your physical state, how much alcohol you drank last night, how much exercise you've taken recently, and so on. *(For more detail about this topic, check out the legendary work of Simons & Chabris[1], or other books on the subject by Daniel J. Levitin[2], Carol Dweck[3], or Richard Wiseman[4].)*

One of the ways in which your mindsets may manifest themselves is in small unconscious instructions, rules or directions you give yourself – little ways in which you tell yourself to look at things one way or another .

This book will explore a few simple but significant possibilities for replacing how you look at things one way with how you could look at things another .

1   Daniel J. Simons & Christopher Chabris, 'Gorillas in our midst: sustained inattentional blindness for dynamic events.' Perception, vol. 28, 1999, p1059–1074 (http://www.wjh.harvard.edu/~cfc/Simons1999.pdf).

2   Daniel J. Levitin, The Organized Mind, Viking, 2015.

3   Carol Dweck, Mindset, Robinson, 2012.

4   Richard Wiseman, Did You Spot The Gorilla?, Arrow, 2004.

Chapter Three

MASCOT™

One thing you should know about us is that we are fond of rubbish mnemonics – crass but simple ways to remember useful stuff.

Our rubbish mnemonic for preparing presentations is MASCOT™. There you go – rubbish! We apologise; it may be rubbish, but strangely, it's very useful for people.

Here's what MASCOT™ stands for:

Materials – stuff I want to bring to illustrate my content and make it interesting.

Audience – what I know about them. What I can guess about them. What they might think about me and my message.

Structure – how to put it all together and in what order. Bits of 'padding' it will need to make it work. 'Tricks' and 'techniques' I will need to engage my audience and keep them engaged.

Content – the key messages. What I actually need to get across.

Objectives – why bother? How do I want to change my

audience (the way they think, their understanding, the action they need to take)?

Tools – what to use to convey my materials: projector, flip charts, pens, tables, chairs, podium, microphone etc.

You might be thinking that materials and tools sound very much like the same thing. We agree. It's a bit odd, because often these two prompts do generate the same things; equally, we find that often they don't. We find that if we don't consider both materials and tools, we'll miss thinking about something important, while when we consider them both, we end up with a more robust piece of thinking.

Chapter Four

The wrong place to begin

It's not helpful, or needed, to put the MASCOT™ elements in an order – which one to consider first, second, third and so on. In reality MASCOT™ provides a thinking prompt, and the elements build on each other – thoughts under one heading should provoke thoughts under another. So it's inappropriate to think about starting in one place and finishing in another.

However, there are a couple of important things to bear in mind.

1. *The last thing to consider.* Many, many people we work with begin planning a presentation by thinking about and getting clear on content. Now, if there is one rule about the order in which to do your thinking, it would be this:

   Content is the wrong place to begin.

   In fact, we recommend a mindset of:

   Content is the last thing to consider

In our experience, when you start putting together a presentation via the content first, it's very easy for other essential thinking about objectives, audience and structure to get crowded out.

We've worked with many people who start planning a presentation by thinking about content; in fact, we've worked with many people who start and finish their planning by thinking about content – content is all they think about. It's possible that the CEO we mentioned in Chapter 1 (the one presenting in New York) constructed a content-led presentation. When you construct a content-led presentation it's like deciding

what I'm going to say before deciding

why I should say anything at all

When you do this, you can end up saying something very, very interesting to a group of people who just aren't interested, or you can end up saying something very, very interesting in a manner which is really, really boring for the people listening.

We've seen some big-time management thinkers and leadership gurus who we know have brilliant and profound things to say (because we've read their books). But in person, delivering a presentation, they don't appear to have thought about *why* this audience is interested – or why this audience *should* be interested. They don't appear to consider *how* to put their content across. And as a result:

- They deliver their content in exactly the way it was written (in the brilliant book). And sadly, in many cases, it doesn't work – it's boring. What was brilliant as a book isn't brilliant when presented in exactly the same way.

Or

- They don't present their book's content in just the way it was written – instead they 'translate' it into a more standard 'presentation' approach; an approach which they believe is required for a presentation. We attended a two-day seminar with one such guru whose work we've loved for years, only to be hugely disappointed by his delivery. In this case, in putting his material into a standard 'presentation' approach he failed to preserve the funky, edgy, innovative style and tone of his book. Somehow, unwittingly, he transformed himself from 'fresh , energetic and persuasive provocateur' into 'boring, predictable, clichéd corporate robot' – what a let-down.

2. *Work on objective and audience early.* Whilst there isn't a hard and fast order, there are some elements to make sure you're working on and getting clear about early on, because they're going to make the biggest difference to your chances of delivering

a great presentation as they're going to make the most impact on your thinking in the other areas. Without question, these elements are objective and audience, closely followed by structure.

By the Way…

In writing this, it would be very easy right now to start working our way through MASCOT™ – starting with materials, then audience etc.

Notice if we did that we'd effectively be delivering a content-led presentation; instead we have an objective, which is to keep you interested, and make you want to read more, so we've decided not to go for the logical, sequential thing. Instead the book will work as follows:

First, at regular intervals we'll break the flow of the text to have a look at some provocative bits of communication theory. These bits of theory are included in order to challenge our assumptions about what makes for good communication, or good presentation.

We anticipate that you will have heard some, if not all, of these before. We want you to consider them here again because we're going to use them to challenge some of our mindsets.

So, in order to get the most out of this book, please notice when you have an automatic response such as:

Yeah, yeah   Heard that before

Know what that's about

Instead, we suggest you actively go for a mindset of:

Let me think about this again

How should this change my next presentation? and

What approach would I take if I took this idea literally?

Second, we'll look at considerations of personal impact — how you make use of you, yourself, as the primary tool for presenting.

And *third*, we will of course work our way through MASCOT™ one step at a time — but we'll do so in order of significance, which is more like:

Objective
Audience
Structure
Materials
Tools
Content

The trouble is, this spells OASMTC — which isn't really a model to remember.

Communication Principle 1 of 5:
The Von Restorff Effect

This principle is named after Hedwig von Restorff (what an outstanding name)!

Is this
Hedwig von
Restorff?   No, it's not; apparently she may have looked

like this   or this   or this

Von Restorff proposed the effect in a paper in 1933. Also referred to as 'the isolation effect' or 'distinctiveness effect', the idea is that items that are different from the context in which they're presented will be more memorable than other items. For example, in a list or sequence of information, an item that stands out from the norm will be more memorable.

Try it out now. Read the list of words below – just the once – then cover them over and try to recall the list.

Twig	Write
Biscuit	Church
Motorway	Ripsnorter
Seaside	Seat
Seat	
Son	

Done it? What did you remember? Probably quite a number of the words. But notice the one that stood out from the others for you; the one you just couldn't forget, not even if you wanted to. This is a demonstration of the von Restorff effect. In presenting terms it's about stand-out moments, stand-out information, stand-out approaches – anything which is discontinuous or different from the rest.

Search the internet for the von Restorff effect and you'll quickly find plenty of images which demonstrate the principle to you.

The von Restorff effect suggests several mindset shifts important in presenting:

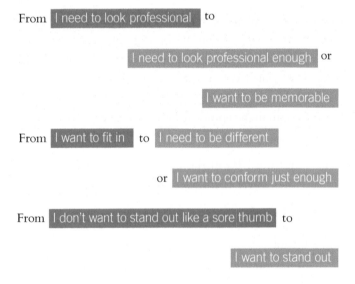

From I need to look professional to

I need to look professional enough or

I want to be memorable

From I want to fit in to I need to be different

or I want to conform just enough

From I don't want to stand out like a sore thumb to

I want to stand out

And mistakes…the idea of making mistakes in presenting is kind of interesting.

From `I'm terrified of making a mistake` to

`Mistakes can be memorable`

What's important is what you do with your mistakes during presentations – the way you respond to your mistakes, and the way you highlight the mistakes you make. With mistakes you choose whether you create a memorable moment that you want, or a memorable moment that you don't want (more on this later).

From `I'm terrified of making a mistake` to

`I can use my mistakes to build rapport` or

`If I handle my mistakes I build credibility`

So, the von Restorff effect should be the cornerstone communication principle in presenting. If your presentation doesn't stand out from the crowd, if it's not memorable, then the danger is that it has no impact.

Of course this isn't necessarily the case if your objective doesn't depend on your presentation being memorable (e.g. if your objective is solely to get a particular decision during the presentation), or if your objective is to make sure your presentation *isn't* memorable (we can't think of an example of this, but there must be one).

Chapter Five

Creating impact 1

We've mentioned already how well we remember one speaker we've seen. But unfortunately, she was memorable in an 'I'm not very interested in you' kind of a way. Whilst we remember that she presented, we don't remember any of her content. On the other hand, many others stand out for wholly positive reasons.

President Bill Clinton was memorable because amidst a sea of PowerPoint presentations, he simply stood behind a lectern and counted out his five key points on the fingers and thumb of one hand. That was the extent of his materials and tools – lectern, lectern mike, himself, fingers and thumb. His presentation was simple, structured, impactful and memorable. We can still count off the five key points of his presentation on our own fingers now – five years later. His Von Restorff Effect was the break from presentational paraphernalia.

When we saw a guy called Patrick Lencioni, he grabbed our attention and our memory in his first fifteen seconds, then maintained it through the next hour or more. His content had to be good to do this, but critically, he'd thought about his audience as much as his content. He knew we'd all been sitting through a conveyor belt of presentations, so he knew he'd have to do something, and keep doing something, to grab us again and again. What he did was simple.

As he introduced himself, standing at the front of the stage (nothing on the projection screen behind him), he described how prone to distraction he could be. As he did so, he broke off, looked up to his right, shouted, "Look – a bird!" and then carried on with his explanation. Silly, but brilliant.

A little later on, in case our attention was beginning to drift, he mentioned his book, asked who wanted a copy and threw it at a raised arm in the audience (a von Restorff moment which he repeated several times throughout his presentation). Seven years later we're still talking about his presentation and his fantastic material regarding the 'five dysfunctions of a team'.

When we saw Nando Parrado present his story of survival in the Andes after the notorious plane crash in 1972, we noticed a distinctly different response from his conference audience. For the first time that day, we stopped scribbling furiously in our notepads, stopped trying to record every detail, stopped noting our observations about what and how he was communicating; we put our pads and pens away, and just sat and listened. When we could tear our attention away enough to glance around the auditorium we saw that all mobile phones had disappeared – no more texting, no more tweeting, no more photos. Everybody was still, four thousand people giving their complete attention to this one person stood alone at the very front of the stage, telling a story accompanied only by a handful of very personal photographs. BAM! What a moment.

These outstanding moments hooked us. These presenters were 'ripsnorter', and we wanted to remember what they said – they knew how to activate their own 'distinctiveness' effect.

Chapter Six

Creating impact 2

Let's check back to one of our opening messages. When faced with this meeting room, most of the people we've worked with on presenting over the last ten years immediately think their presentations should look like this:

Now, in terms of the Von Restorff Principle, the personal memorability and impact of your presentation is likely to be very low. Compared to others delivered in the same meeting or on the same day, it's likely that many of them (if not all of them) are going to look like this. That's right – you know those meetings where we all sit facing the same way all day long, facing the same wall, looking at the same screen, on which are displayed similar graphics and pictures, in a similar style – those meetings! The ones where everybody is 'professional'. The ones unconsciously designed to help us become bored, hypnotised even, or cynical and overly critical. The ones which induce too much cognitive strain, keep us at the office too late, and fail to help us process the onslaught of information we've 'got to get through today'.

So, let's start thinking about your personal impact immediately. What if you didn't assume the above presentation style when faced with this room? What if you considered some others?

If you feel under-confident, or you feel exposed stood in front of a group, get out of the spotlight – let them look at your visuals.

From the back you can pause, hold the silence and enjoy it.

Promote engagement and encourage discussion.

Again, get out of the spotlight, put the focus onto your content, and encourage your audience to take responsibility for the thinking.

Change the state of your audience.

If they're tired, get them breathing again, and get them engaged again.

Refreshingly simple.

Take away the pressure for a big performance.

Deliver a straightforward, and personal message.

It's the thinking we get from the elements of MASCOT™ which will help us to decide which of these approaches we might go for, and when.

None of these of course are 'wacky' or 'out there' – they're essentially very conformist. Critically though, they're a little different. And each has its own benefits.

First published in Psychological Review (vol. 63, p81–97, 1956), George Miller's famous idea is about the limitations of short-term memory.

Miller's proposal is that the short-term memory seems to be able to receive, process and remember a very small number of chunks of information. A chunk of information is, in part, determined by the receiver of the information, e.g. if you receive a short sentence in a language you understand it's probable that you'll treat the sentence as a chunk of information; whereas if you receive a short sentence in a language which you don't understand, you may receive and process only parts of that sentence – an individual word or sound may count as a chunk.

This idea is often translated into the notion that people can receive, process and remember between five and nine chunks of information. We're not suggesting here that this is factually the case – a short search of the internet will turn up much discussion and further research about a short-term memory buffer of four chunks or even less.

What we are suggesting is that as a mindset for preparing and delivering presentations, the idea that your audience might only cope with five to nine chunks is stimulating and useful.

It's important to remember that this represents five to nine 'raw' chunks of information, i.e. nothing has been done to increase their memorability. As we proceed we'll consider other communication principles which suggest that presenters might be able to stretch this number, using different techniques and structures for their presentation.

Remember our description of President Bill Clinton? He had five clear points – one for each digit on his hand. He discussed details around each one, but he kept coming back to the clarity of the five. And our brains coped with this just fine – more than coped; we could remember his messages with ease, and still do.

There are some common mindsets which regularly crop up when we talk to people who don't feel confident about presenting – mindsets which George Miller's Magic Number 7 should challenge:

I've got twenty minutes to fill (and I must fill them)   vs.

What are my five to nine key points?

so   How long will it take me to cover them?

I must cover enough content to be credible   vs.

They'll only get five to nine no matter how much I do

so   Doing the job with less is credible (more so)

I can't run out of steam – I'll look stupid   vs.

I shouldn't waffle on – I'll be boring

and   Extra content is only a distraction

The very real stress about 'filling the time I've been given' with content is limiting and scary for many people; ironically, those of us who feel this stress are just as likely as our colleagues to deliver long presentations, thus contributing to long meeting days in which we all have to listen to material and information which we won't remember, which is boring us rigid, which we've heard before, and which is keeping us stuck in the room while we know that the work is piling up at our desk.

Do everyone a favour: begin with a mindset of five to nine key points, nail your presentation with the information that's needed, and don't compulsively add more because you feel you have to demonstrate that you've done as much as the other robots. Imagine what it would be like if everyone did this; if everyone just got their point over, kept back the detail when it wasn't needed, and delivered shorter, more memorable messages!

Kill the robot in you.

Get the meeting done quicker.

Let's go home on time for a change.

Chapter Seven

Objectives

The objectives of your presentation are really important, but they can be quite tricky to get a grip of – unless you're really lucky. It's unlikely you'll be able to define your objectives straight off; much more likely that you'll get an initial idea of an objective, and that it'll evolve as you consider and work on the other MASCOT™ elements.

When we ask people to tell us their objective for a meeting they're running, a presentation they're delivering, or frankly, a communication interaction of any kind, often we get other things in response, such as:

- Agenda items.
- Content.
- Corporate buzzwords like 'engagement' and 'motivation'.

Or we get something objective-like but passive – something which won't really achieve much:

- "To give an update."
- "To pass on *this* information."
- "To keep them in the loop."

Of course, these kinds of things might be fine. But double-check – when we come up with these kinds of non-objectives we know we need to consider again what it is we're really after. We challenge ourselves with a few quick questions, such as:

- Why not just send an email then?
- What is it about this information that means they have to hear me say it, and see me move while I say it?
- Why not just issue a handout and let everybody read it? "There – that's my presentation!" (What a result that might be for everyone concerned!)
- Why not send a pre-read with some guidance about what to do with it?

These sorts of questions lead to answers which are much more active, e.g.:

- "Well, they've heard this message before, but they haven't acted upon it."
- "This isn't about the information – it's about giving them the opportunity to ask questions about the information, so they can make decisions and take action."
- "They didn't do what they said they would the last time they heard it – so this time I'll make sure they do!"
  Or even:
- "This essential information is so boring and impenetrable that nobody will ever absorb it properly unless they're trapped in a little room with me and a bunch of their peers for twenty minutes and made to digest it properly somehow." (So I'd better work out how to do that.)

Notice how these later answers are lurching towards an active objective. They might lead us to a presentation objective as simple as:

- "To get them moving."
- "To get them committed to action."
- "To wake them up."
- "To stir the pot."
- "To get on with it, or to stop talking about it altogether."
- "To get to an honest conversation about whether this is really relevant or not."
- "To remove barriers to acceptance by answering their questions."
- "To get everybody on the same page in the shortest time possible."
- "To sell them on my recommendations."
- "To enthuse and excite them."
- "To make them see things in a completely different way so that we can make changes."

You can see how many of these objectives are about the audience, rather than about what the content is supposed to drive, and many are not about the content at all. Notice how these are much more productive objectives for a presentation. They will begin to generate in us more challenging thoughts about *how* to do the presentation (structure), and how to engage each person or each group of people (audience and structure).

So, get yourself an objective – and get it early.

Of course, you're not always the person who's decided that you need to present. Often, it's your boss, a key stakeholder, or a customer of yours who decides you need to present. And this means that it's really them who defines the objective (or fails to define the objective).

It's very easy to accept *someone else's* lousy objective as *your* objective. And it's particularly tempting to accept it if that person is your boss or somebody 'important' or 'powerful'. When presented with a lousy objective by somebody 'important' we'll ask one or two key questions:

- "What's this all about?"
- "What are you hoping will happen as a result of this?"
- "What do you want?"
- "And if you get that, what will that do for you?"

This'll get them thinking about their objective.

Actually, go easy on them – they might not have an objective themselves. Be prepared to realise that they too are just running an undeclared robot programme in their head: *we'll have a presentation, because that's what we do.*

You could ask a few of the people who are going to be at the meeting – those who'll be listening to your presentation – the same questions as above.

44

Again, be careful with this, and guard against creating the impression that you're going to deliver a presentation to please everybody. You're just gathering information, trying to work out what's required.

And don't discount yourself – ask yourself:

- "What do I want?"
- "And if I get that, what will it do for me?"

Some people forget this one – they think they're trying to satisfy everybody else, and they assume, for some reason, that it's not appropriate for them to deliver their presentation to satisfy themselves in some way (strange, but a common occurrence).

You might come up with something like:

- "To change the way they see me."
- "To build my credibility."
- "To stand out from the crowd."

So, you might end up with at least two objectives for your presentation – one to do with the stated purpose of the presentation and one that you keep to yourself (an objective just for you).

Recently we were working with a senior director who, when asked what he wanted from a meeting he was about to begin, said, "I need to understand what's going on, set my expectations for what happens next and assess whether this person is bought in to the change or not."

We pushed him several times to get clearer – "What do you really *want*, though?"

Finally, after much to-ing and fro-ing, he said, "I want to hit him hard so that he wakes up, talks straight and cuts out the usual flannel." Now that's an objective. He realised that he had to push himself to be clear about what he really wanted. And we all do. It's very easy for us to be too vague or come up with corporate cliché or hot air when preparing a meeting, a presentation or a communication.

So, in order to come up with objectives for your presentation which are helpful and meaningful, the big distinction is really about moving from passive mindsets to active mindsets. Let's look at a few more examples. Some on the list below require clear choices – which one am I going for? – whilst others represent more of balance to be struck; i.e. in any given presentation you might need to move from one to the other and back again.

Be seen as professional and

Make an impact

Reinforce the current situation and

Make something change

Promote harmony and

Flush out disagreements

Keep things comfortable and

Challenge them

Change the way they see this topic and

Change the way they see me

Match their expectations and

Mismatch their expectations

Conform and

Conform enough

Some of these mindsets come up again when we think about structure. Remember, we don't need to think of each of the MASCOT™ elements in isolation – one will immediately inform another, e.g. if you choose a mindset that your presentation needs to:

Change the way they see this topic and

Change the way they see me and

Pin down some actions

then your objective will need to reflect this, but your structure also will need to reflect this – you'll need to do something in the way you present the content to achieve this. And of course, you'll need to understand your audience properly – you'll need to have a good idea (or even a guess if nothing else) about how they might currently see the topic, and how they might currently see you.

Communication Principle 3 of 5:
Primacy and Recency

Laughably simple, this one. In articles dating from 1885 (Memory: A Contribution to Experimental Psychology), Hermann Ebbinghaus described the 'serial position effect'. The idea is that, when presented with a blob of data or information, people will tend to pick up and remember the first stuff they saw and heard, and the last stuff they saw and heard. According to this idea, graphically, the way that people absorb information presented to them across a session looks like this:

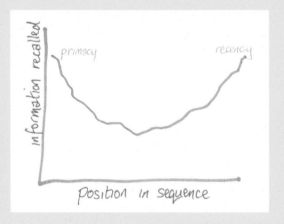

Something different happens in terms of the way we process information in the middle of a presentation. We don't need to get too concerned here with exactly what that is; whether people's attention wanders or their brains start processing what they've already heard – we just need to be aware that the information in the middle is at risk, and that the information at the beginning and the end had better be important stuff which you want people to remember.

So, consider *primacy and recency effects* and check a few of your mindsets.

Start with your agenda

Start with something you really want them to remember e.g. the five or more key points themselves (not an introduction to them)

Tell 'em what you're going to tell 'em, tell 'em, then tell 'em what you told 'em

End with something you really want them to remember A restatement of recommendations, instead of key points

Recently we had another lovely demonstration of this wonderful idea. We were just finishing day one of a three-day development workshop. Mark had just signed off the day with a quick run back through the key ideas covered, and a "That's it – goodnight everyone, see you in the morning." As the group began to gather their belongings and put on their coats to leave, Doug called them over to stand around a model which we'd displayed on the wall and intended to talk about on day two, but hadn't discussed so far. With a mischievous glint in his eye, he announced that he was going to give them one last idea and proceeded to run through this model with an attitude of "It doesn't matter whether you get this or not." Within sixty seconds (much too fast!), it was done and Doug told the group again that the day was over and to have a good evening.

During our first chat with the group on the morning of day two, one participant reported that she'd awoken suddenly at 3am that morning with a model in her head, and that she could remember six out of seven of the concepts contained in that idea, but that she'd lain awake for a long time trying to remember the seventh concept.

Of course, you know already which model she couldn't get out of her head. It was the one Doug had thrown into the mix at the very last moment. Without any conscious instruction to do so, her brain was fixed on this idea and actively processing for information about it – almost against her will. How annoyingly useful for her learning.

Chapter Eight

Audience – the big one!

Yep, there's no getting away from it – this is the big one! When you're presenting you're always presenting *to somebody*, so it's unlikely that you'll be as effective as you could be unless you've engaged with who they are, and you know a little something about them. Yet, we see it all the time: people presenting, or planning to present, not having thought about it enough – or at all. Consider it now, in relation to a presentation you'll be delivering in the next few days or weeks – what do you know about:

- The audience you're presenting to?
- What this audience thinks about the topic you're going to present?
- What the audience thinks about you, the presenter?
- What the audience thinks about the meeting which your presentation is a part of?
- How the audience will feel physically and mentally by the time you begin to present?
- Which members of the audience are likely to support proposals you're going to make?
- Which audience members are likely to oppose proposals you're going to make?

- Who in the audience holds the power and influence?
- Who in the audience is known to be tricky or difficult?
- What these people think about presentations generally?
- What they'll be expecting a presentation about this topic to be like, and how many times they may have sat through it before?
- What they'll be expecting a presentation from you to be like?

Many of these will affect which of the mindset balances you should go for from those listed at the end of the last chapter.

A lot of people we work with don't like doing this; they put it off or avoid it, they don't want to start thinking about the audience to whom they're going to present, and it seems to prompt all kinds of difficult, challenging mindsets in them which they don't like, e.g.:

I want to feel positive about my presentation

Thinking about my audience will make me feel negative

I don't want to feel negative about my presentation

I want to stay relaxed about my presentation

Thinking about my audience will make me feel nervous

I don't want to feel nervous about my presentation

I don't have time for this amount of analysis

I'll do it nearer the time, once I've got my content sorted

I don't have access to my audience

I don't know my audience   I can't plan for my audience

Too many people – I can't please everyone

They just don't like me – so there's nothing I can do

Let's address a particularly significant mindset choice:

From Thinking about my audience will make me feel negative

and I don't want to feel negative about my presentation

to Negative thinking is productive in the planning step

Let's be really clear on this one. We think of preparing for a presentation in two distinct steps – the planning step and the pre-check step.

Step 1 - Planning
This is about *it* – the presentation.
Key mindsets here are:

Preparing the presentation is everything

Enough time and attention are crucial

Step 2 - Pre-Check

This is about *me* – the primary tool I'll use to deliver my presentation. Key mindsets here are:

Preparing myself is everything

If I haven't prepared well enough I can still nail it if I sort myself out

If I've over-prepared I can still nail it if I sort myself out

Step 1 - Planning

The larger proportion of this book focuses on this step. It's where the volume of the work is – getting clear about what your presentation is for, how to put it together, how to structure it, how to deliver it, planning the materials and tools to use to get the best result, writing the content etc. All of this is designed to meet your objective and the needs of your audience (as well as some of their wants).

Step 2 - Pre-Check

This one doesn't take much time, but it can make a disproportionate contribution to your chances of success. This step is done once all your planning is finished. You'll need to do it a number of times on the day you're going to deliver your presentation – probably once or twice in the hours before, and again just before you begin. This step is quite different – knowing that everything to do with the presentation itself is complete (or not complete), this step is about *me* (not about *it*), and it's about you getting yourself into the state and mindset to deliver to your best ability. So here you'll focus on *you* (rather than the presentation) and how *you* want to be – how *you* need to be.

It's important to clearly separate the two steps. For example, negativity has radically different implications in each step.

Negative thinking is productive in the planning step

Negative thinking is essential in the planning step

In the planning step it's important to engage with all the potential 'negative' responses and reactions which you might get from your audience.

Forewarned is forearmed

If I can predict the negative reactions, I can design some tools or something structurally to deal with them

Negative thinking isn't so helpful in your pre-check step. In this step it's important for you to develop a productive state – a positive state; a 'me at my best' state, knowing that you're fully prepared (or knowing that you're not, and it's too late now to let that affect you and your performance).

Now, with regard to the planning step you might already be objecting:

I don't have time for this amount of analysis

We agree – you don't have time for much analysis. This isn't about knowing everything – the planning step is about making good enough predictions about the range of responses you might get from your audience, given who's in the room.

It's not much time – It's thinking, not research

Squeeze your time!

This really is a thinking discipline rather than a research one – you can know very little about your audience and still jump to some useful conclusions about the range of responses you'll get. And of course, you don't want to know too much because you're not going to design a presentation which is built around these potential 'worst' responses – that would be a self-fulfilling prophecy. Instead you're going to come up with little structural tricks and tools – approaches to presenting – which are designed to deal with these things *if* they come up; tricks and tools which you may not even need to include in your presentation if they don't.

Of course, if you have some time and the presentation is big enough and important enough you might want to do a little research – you might speak to a few people who'll be attending your presentation. But go carefully with this – if you do this too well, you can drift towards writing a presentation designed to meet everyone else's needs, and this can make for a very bland message, and can result in you losing the strong message you want to put across.

The idea that:

This is a thinking discipline (rather than research)

should also deal with difficult mindsets like:

I don't have access to my audience

I don't know my audience   I can't plan for my audience

So, whilst it might be nice to talk to a few representatives of your audience, if you can't, you can get enough of what you need from a conversation with one key person – someone who knows the population. Or just guess, but make your guesses educated ones, on the basis of who the population are, their length of service, the kind of roles they've been doing, the amount of change they've been through recently, how they've been treated by the organisation.

And when you practise this thinking discipline, you should be considering the kinds of issues listed at the head of this chapter:

- Who's in the room?
- What do they think of me? (Good and bad – and what's the worst?)
- What do they think of the topic? (Good, bad and worst?)
- What will they think of my recommendations?
- What concerns might they have?

- What will be their outright objections to what I'm saying?
- Who are the experts on this topic?
- What do people need, based on what I know about them?
- What do they think they want (by comparison)?

All of this should loop straight back into objectives – answers to any of these questions should immediately prompt thoughts such as:

- So how do I want to change the way they think?
- So how should my key messages fit with what they know?

Communication Principle 4 of 5: the Zeigarnik Principle

This is about how useful interruptions are to memory, communication and learning due to the way in which they encourage us to hold on to and process information in our short-term memory (waiting for the interruption to end). Far from causing problems, interruptions, distractions and pauses can help communication.

So the story goes, it's 1927 and Bluma Zeigarnik and her mentor Kurt Lewin are in a café one day, when they notice and begin to discuss how waiters and waitresses seem to be able to hold a quantity of information in their short-term memories – who ordered what, at what table, and where they're sitting. This information remains in their short-term memories until each respective table's order is complete and the party leaves the café – at which point the information is 'dumped' from the waiter/waitress' short-term memory.

This controversial idea, which continues to be the subject of much discussion, was studied and written up by Zeigarnik.

In *On Finished and Unfinished Tasks* (Über das Behalten von erledigten und unerledigten Handlungen), Bluma Zeigarnik, *Psychologische Forschung*, 1927. 9, Zeigarnik describes how her experiments indicate that unfinished tasks are remembered better than completed ones. Or in this case, the implication is that a piece of communication which is interrupted or unfinished is remembered better than a completed one. The mind continues to process the information until it's deemed complete. Whether you're convinced by this theory or not, as a mindset for thinking about presenting, and as a provocative idea with which to change the way we look at presenting, the Zeigarnik Principle offers some tantalising possibilities.

Silence is bad – it will ruin my credibility

vs. Silence is good – pauses help my communication

or Silence is great! My listeners' brains are continuing to process my content in the silence

Mistakes are terrible

vs. Mistakes can be 'good interruptions', promoting recall

or What I do with mistakes is what counts – making them positive pauses is what counts

I have to get my whole message across

vs. Lack of completion can be productive

In our experience, silence and something going wrong are often people's big worries about presenting. So, put these worries into your planning step. Know that something is going to go wrong! The microphone *will* stop working, the projector *will* stop responding; you *will* forget the point you want to make. Know that this is going to happen, and plan for it – decide what you'll do and say, but above all decide you're not going to apologise over and over for it or make an excruciating joke about it. Know that a pause is not an awkward silence unless you do something to generate the awkwardness. Know that a pause and a silence are going to help your presentation, and make you look even more credible if you handle them well. We've worked with many people who've decided what they'll do if the microphone or the projector stops working (they'll stand there and calmly tell the audience that it's happened and ask for someone to come and fix it). Remarkably, on most occasions where we've coached someone about this, the most common feedback they get about their presentation is about "the amazing way you dealt with that technical hitch – I wish I could do that. You're so confident!"

If something goes wrong, I'll look like a fool

vs. If something goes wrong, it'll be an opportunity to build my credibility

Remember, the Zeigarnik Principle suggests that inter-ruptions, distractions, mistakes, silences, pauses – all these things are good and useful for the effective communica-tion of information. But if you start getting in the way of this by drawing attention to your mistakes, giving them more prominence than the content of your presentation, drawing attention to them again and again with too many embarrassed apologies, this will undermine your commu-nication. This is the thing that will make you look foolish.

What if someone interrupts?!

vs. Interruptions are useful for memory and retention

and What I do with interruptions is what counts

I don't want questions until the end – they'll interrupt my flow vs. Questions aren't a problem – they might help me convey my message

Using questions; responding at the right moment is what's important

This brings us back to the significance of negativity. Whilst it's not helpful during the pre-check step, negativity is very helpful at the planning step, but it needs a particular mindset shift:

from I really hope nothing goes wrong to

Things will go wrong – guaranteed!

and What's going to go wrong? Let me plan what I'll do

Most people seem to think they ought to be able to cope with mistakes and things going wrong in their presentations automatically without having planned for them. This is unrealistic. But of course, once you know they might happen, and once you've decided what you'll do or say if they happen, then you're ready to deal with them – you're ready to stay unruffled, impressive and credible.

Now, once you've embraced the positive possibilities of mistakes and silences, you can move on to considering the Zeigarnik Principle as a *deliberate* tool for you to build into your presentations. You can consider – what can I do with this idea in terms of the structure of my presentation?

Chapter Nine

Structure

Here are some simplistic definitions of structure:

- What to do at the beginning, in the middle, and at the end.
- What to do in what order.
- The flow of content – how you communicate your content.
- Ways to communicate so that your audience is more likely to engage with your content in the way you want throughout your presentation (things you could do to mix it up a bit – remember Patrick Lencioni: 'I'll throw a copy of my book into the audience five times during my presentation').
- How much time to give to each of my main sections or topics.

So issues of structure will include:

- Sequencing of ideas, to help your audience absorb each one more easily, e.g. if you applied Communication Principle 3: Primacy and Recency to your structure, then you might start with a key idea or a piece of information which you want to land (rather than beginning with an introduction). Similarly, you might be brave enough to save a critical idea for the very last moment of your presentation.

- Moments or pieces which aren't needed in order to communicate your content; instead they're designed to affect the state of your audience in some way:
  - Typically, a good introduction is designed to do this — it's designed to enable your audience to get themselves ready for your message; to break their state and their thinking from the previous session, so that they're ready for yours.
  - The cringeworthy 'ice-breaker' is another example. We don't like this because it's so difficult to get right, and often so clichéd that it sets a tone of cringeworthiness which is all too memorable.
- Moments to build in to break up the flow of ideas. Again, this is to help your audience process the information you're providing, e.g. if you applied Communication Principle 4: the Zeigarnik Principle, then you'd make more of this. For example, you would:
  - Pause more deliberately between ideas.
  - Break off from your presentation to take a comment from an audience member.
  - Tell a short story which isn't needed.
  - Make a humorous comment about some random detail from your visual aids.

- Look out of the window and draw your audience's attention to something happening outside, etc.

  (Of course to do this you'll need to feel like you have a little spare time in your presentation – you'll need to make sure you haven't planned so much content that you need all the time available. And to help you with this, you'll need to remember Communication Principle 2: George Miller's Magic Number 7 and the mindsets that go with it).

- Activities or 'sessions' which are not needed to communicate your content; instead they're designed to change *your* state, as the presenter, e.g. sometimes presenters will play a piece of music designed to get their audience in the right mood. It's equally valid to play a piece of music for *you* – something to get *you* in the right state.

We saw a presentation by Robert Dilts (a hero of ours). He used several quotes from Einstein and Gandhi in his presentation. One of his audience on the day asked him why he was doing this (the inference was 'We don't need you to do this, Robert – you don't need to prove you know so much'). He calmly explained that quoting these people wasn't for the benefit of the audience – it was for him. When saying, "Einstein said this", or "Gandhi said that", for him it was like gathering his friends around him to give him strength and confidence; creating for him the sense that 'Einstein and Gandhi have got my back'.

- Moments to insert in order to grab your audience's attention in a particular way, and get them engaged again (maybe to help them wake up and prepare to concentrate again).

- Activities or 'sessions' which are not needed to communicate your content; instead they're deliberately designed to change the state of your audience in some way, to make them think differently so that they're ready to consider your content, or to develop a particular state in them so they engage with your content in that way.

Once we saw a presentation by Paul Krugman. We hadn't heard of him before. He was introduced on stage as "one of the world's foremost economists". Probably like a few others in his audience that day, we had distinct mindsets as he came on stage:

> This'll be dry   This'll be boring   This'll be difficult
>
> I won't keep up with this

As he began his presentation he projected an incredibly complicated graph onto the screen behind him. There were so many squiggly lines on this graph, those of us in the audience with worries about dryness, difficulty and not being able to keep up sank into our chairs ready to be baffled, ready to switch off, ready for a doze.

He waited for five minutes before he pointed to the graph and said, "Those of you who are looking at the graph behind me, I'd better explain – I'm not intending to talk about it. We don't really need it – it's interesting enough, but to be honest

---

68

I've only put it up there for those of you who know that economists present very complicated data and ideas, and for those of you who want the proof that I am a real economist. Otherwise, it's kind of irrelevant."

Well, the state change in us, and in the audience, was instant – people visibly sat up straighter and paid attention again. We engaged as if we could dare to understand what the Nobel Prize-winning economist was going to say, and the two of us were rewarded with one of the clearest, most stimulating and provocative presentations we've ever seen and heard. And now, years later, we still remember his key messages and are always interested in what he has to say.

What a great example of the use of a bit of 'structure' thinking – *given what my audience might be thinking about a presentation from me, let me build in something to my structure to change their state early on, so that they can relax and engage with my message.* It wouldn't have worked so well if he'd done this right at the beginning – structurally he needed to lull us into the state of 'dry', 'boring' and 'difficult' first in order to break it and create the state we needed for a great session.

As you can tell from all the examples above, as soon as you're considering your audience, this should drag your thinking into issues of structure, and this should follow on to materials and tools.

Finally, objections: As part of your planning step, when considering your audience, you should be listing the kinds of objections or concerns they might raise – in preparation for one presentation we delivered, we covered an A4 sheet of paper with the possible objections. Once you predict your list of possibilities, then you can plan what you should be doing structurally to deal with them, e.g.:

- You could declare the objections you expect openly and early in your presentation; then:
  - Address them all in one go.

  Or
  - Ask which ones they agree with, and tailor the rest of your presentation to address only these.

  Or
  - Explain how this presentation is not designed to address these, but *is* designed to flush out others so that all can be dealt with in the near future.

- Or you could explain that you're expecting some objections so you've reserved some time at the end of your presentation to discuss these.

- You could explain that you know there will be objections (maybe even that there should be objections), but that this is not the session in which to discuss them, and that you'll be emailing all attendees afterwards to gather these.

- You could have a 'parking board' to hand, on the wall, and simply record objections (or get somebody else to record them) as they arise – thanking each 'objector' as you go, explaining that you'll take these away to address. (Of course, we're calling them objections, but you don't need to label them this way during your presentation – *issues* or *discussion points* will do the job.)

We've seen all of these approaches, and used them successfully ourselves. Again, the point here is that as soon as you're engaged with your audience, and the range of responses they might have to your presentation, then you have to begin coming up with structural motifs that you plan to use to deal with them. (If you want another example of a bit of structure which is not needed to communicate content, but is inserted specifically to deal with potential objections that an audience might be making, then look back at pages 14 and 15 – we were doing it ourselves with those pages).

Thinking about this stuff as part of your structure means that you're able to have some control over the situation – and that's good!

Here are a few more specific examples of bits of structure – activities and sessions – which aren't needed in order to communicate your content, but are designed to change the state of your audience in some way:

- Discussion pairs – two minutes for people to talk to their neighbour about a detail you've presented. This might be designed only to change their state, e.g. if they've been sitting listening to speakers for some time and you want to give them a chance to wake up again.
- Get them up out of their chairs to consider material which you've displayed on the walls (great for re-oxygenating their brains, waking them up, and taking the focus off you).

- Present your materials on the table in front of them, and position yourself amongst them (as in the photo in Chapter 6). This could be to meet an objective of getting everybody into the same way of thinking, or to deal with anticipated hostility towards you or your topic.

- Present your materials on the wall away from the overhead screen (again as in the photo in Chapter 6). This could be designed to wake the audience up, get them closer to you (metaphorically as well as physically), increase their rapport with you by having them follow you physically, and begin breaking down barriers by making the presentation less formal and more open for discussion.

- Invite members of the audience to come and stand by your presentation when they're discussing certain details (whilst you become part of the audience) – again, this is designed to move ownership of messages from you to them.

- Put up your first slide, then quietly move to the back of the room, behind your audience. Don't say anything until they've read it. Let the silence hang there. Enjoy the moment as their mindset shifts and their collective state changes.

- Put up your first slide. Make it the one they're expecting to see (the one they've seen time and again before). Leave it for a few seconds, then turn the projector off, look at your audience and ask them a provocative question like "So what's the real issue here?" That'll shake them out of their hypnotised state.

- Get them out of their seats and ask them to follow

you out of the room. Deliver your opening message in that space (e.g. in the corridor) and then take them back in. This is a technique we've used many times ourselves and it always creates some kind of 'frisson' or state change.

Some of these will seem risky to you.

They are.

Remember, they're only examples of things you might try in response to specific challenges.

Don't compulsively shove them into every presentation you do – in fact, don't compulsively shove them into *any* presentation you do. Remember, this is all about considering your audience early on in your planning, and then making strong decisions about what to do *on this particular occasion, for this particular audience.*

Communication Principle 5 of 5:
Cognitive Ease

In his wonderful book *Thinking Fast and Slow*, Daniel Kahneman explains how, as humans, we are predisposed to favour thinking which is easy. He describes this as the difference between cognitive ease and cognitive strain. Referring to a series of studies and examples, he illustrates how communications which induce in us a sense of cognitive ease will be trusted, believed, and even taken as the truth above communications which induce a sense of cognitive strain. Even when there appears to be no qualitative difference between two pieces of information, we'll favour as true the piece of information which is made easier for us to process.

Kahneman cites a number of examples of ways in which information can be communicated to induce cognitive ease:

- Information printed in a clear font.[5]
- Information which is repeated.[6]
- Information for which we've been primed.[7] Priming takes many forms; some simple examples would be:
  - Being told there are five key points to the message, so that we look out for them.
  - Being told that point three of the message is most important (then listening in anticipation and watching while the speaker counts off points one and two on their fingers).

---

5 Daniel Kahneman, Thinking Fast and Slow, 2011, Chapter 5, p63.
6 Daniel Kahneman, Thinking Fast and Slow, 2011, Chapter 5, p62.
7 Daniel Kahneman, Thinking Fast and Slow, 2011, Chapter 4, p52–58.

- Being shown an apparently random piece of information upfront, like a list of key words – "These will be the key words in this presentation." (Now our attention will look for those words throughout the communication.)
- Using simpler language.[8]
- Making information memorable (e.g. an idea told in rhyme has been shown to be judged more insightful than the same idea told without rhyme)[9]. Information which is easy to read or to pronounce (e.g. if you quote a source, Kahneman's advice is to choose one with a name that's easy to pronounce – people will give it more credence if it is).[10]
- Information which is presented to people when they're in a good mood. (The sense of well-being encourages cognitive ease and easier processing of information – again, people are more likely to trust information when they're in a good mood[11], so structurally you might introduce something only designed to get the audience into a good mood.)

As usual with the communication principles we're covering here, these ideas are relevant to some very familiar and regularly occurring mindset choices in people who are presenting:

8 Daniel Kahneman, Thinking Fast and Slow, 2011, Chapter 5, p63.
9 Daniel Kahneman, Thinking Fast and Slow, 2011, Chapter 5, p63
10 Daniel Kahneman, Thinking Fast and Slow, 2011, Chapter 5, p64.
11 Daniel Kahneman, Thinking Fast and Slow, 2011, Chapter 5, p69.

I must present all the information required

vs. Too much information may induce cognitive strain

and Keep it simple

I must fill the time I've got

vs. I repeat my key messages many times

and I need less content than the time available

I can't run out of steam – I'll look stupid

vs. Extra content could increase analysis (cognitive strain)

and Less really can be more

Graphs and graphics need to be complete

vs. Relevant information is all that's needed

and Present simplicity
(have the detail available when asked)

I mustn't bore people

vs. I need time to repeat key messages

and Seven times is the magic number

The objective for your presentation is very important again here: if in presenting, you're really selling an idea (making a recommendation) which you want to be accepted, then cognitive ease is helpful, so beware of overcomplicating your message.

If in presenting you want your audience to accept your point of view, again cognitive ease is helpful.

Political campaign managers and persuasive orators are familiar with this idea. However, cognitive strain in your audience is not always a bad thing: if you haven't come to an opinion about your topic, if you're not trying to convince your audience of a particular message, then cognitive strain – a sense of questioning and analytical processing of the information you're presenting – might be useful. If you want to generate thinking in your audience, then whilst signals of cognitive ease are useful, keeping it simple may not be what you're after.

Chapter Ten

Structure – the broad flow of content

In our experience people spend much of their planning time worrying about the flow of content – what to say first, second and third in order that their presentation makes sense, and so that it creates impact and is as persuasive as possible.

This is understandable – the flow of ideas is of major importance. It's possibly the second or third most important aspect of designing a presentation. However, there isn't such a need to invest so heavily in this decision. You can minimise the amount of time and brain-work it takes you to come up with the best structure, because there are plenty of straightforward, tried and tested communication structures already available. You can just take the best one off the shelf to do the particular job required, depending on the audience and objectives involved.

Here are a few examples:

- BOMM – a planning tool commonly used in Fast Moving Consumer Goods (FMCG) sales environments.

- GROW – the classic coaching model.
- Sell – there are many versions of word patterns (or verbal structures) used in 'selling'; just find one that is structured to build the persuasiveness of an argument. This will probably provide you with a really neat option for a presentation.

You can track down plenty more example structures on the internet.

Let's have a look at how these first few work.

BOMM

Background – what's the history of this issue, what's the current situation, what are the limitations and constraints, and as a result, what are the needs which are to be satisfied?
Objective – what do we want? What are we trying to achieve? What's the outcome?
Methods – what are my proposals for how we go about this?
Measurement – how will we know if we've succeeded and when?

GROW

(You'll notice that this is very similar to BOMM, with a couple of elements rearranged. And of course, this rearrangement can change the message quite profoundly.)

Goal – what do we want? What are we trying to achieve? What's the outcome?

Reality – where are we up to (by comparison)? What have we tried so far? What's worked and what hasn't worked? What are the current proposals still to be implemented?

Options – what could we do? What are the ideas to be considered?

Wrap Up – what will we do? (These are akin to recommendations, with timescales and names of those responsible as needed.)

Sell

Here's our preferred verbal structure for 'selling' – it makes a fine structure for a presentation. As you'll notice, there are once again some common elements between this and BOMM/GROW:

Summarise the Situation – what's the history of this issue, what's the current situation, what are the limitations and constraints, and as a result, what are the needs which are to be satisfied?

State the Idea – this is my proposal.

Describe How it Works – to make this happen we'll do this, then we'll do that, followed by this...

Benefits – list the benefits of taking this approach.

Close – some statements designed to get agreement to proceed, which might include a proposal for a plan, timescales and the names of those responsible.

The fact that there are some critical similarities between these structures (which are designed for different activities) should give us heart that there are some core parts of any piece of communication which we can assume are useful in most presentations. If you can get a number of these types of structures in your head (which is easily achieved), you can just plug the right one in at the right moment. Another benefit of this is that your structure can suggest levels of content, e.g. if you're putting together a PowerPoint presentation using BOMM or GROW, this immediately suggests four slides for your presentation, whereas Sell suggests five slides. In this way, you can quickly get clarity early on in your planning.

Once you're confident with these structures, you can easily play mix and match between them to achieve the simple structure you need for the particular situation.

Chapter Eleven

Structure – the little bits and pieces

We've dealt with plenty of structural stuff already, but let's recap some communication principles we've described, thinking about these in terms of little bits and pieces of structure that could help.

Primacy and Recency

Pay attention to the first and last messages you present. Too many people we work with begin with a load of waffle: "My name is…, and I've been asked to give a presentation about…" (Primacy moment gone!) In a management report it's normal to expect an 'executive summary' upfront – you could go for the same thing here: a really short version of your key point or recommendation. You might follow this with a bit of introductory blather, to allow people to recover before you present your content in full.

The Magic Number 7

Be careful with how much information you're trying to cram into your presentation. It's the law of diminishing returns: it's possible that the more you add in, the less will land. A strong and simple discipline here is to write your presentation a first time, then have another look – brutally checking for the seven to nine key ideas that you've got to get across. Remember, you can always keep a huge amount of detail and further points 'off the table' – in your bag, ready to be introduced should you need them.

Remember, the five to nine principle is about the number of chunks. A good presenter will present more than nine pieces of information but they'll find ways to group together these pieces so that there remain less than seven 'chunks' overall for us to focus on and remember. As they do this, they'll indicate *how ideas are grouped*, even giving names to each chunk or group. Then they'll keep repeating the name of each chunk (as opposed to all the detail of each chunk).

Cognitive Ease: Repetition

If you listen to motivational speakers like Zig Ziglar you'll hear them doing this to an extent that lesser presenters might consider embarrassing. Remember that people can start to believe a message is true simply because it is repeated. Presenters who repeat skilfully in this manner are hypnotising their listeners with the key points of their presentation; the challenge is how to forget the key messages rather than how to remember them.

 ## Outstanding Moments

Somehow you have to marshal these moments. Plan one or two into your presentation – some common ways to do this would include:

- Silly pictures to illustrate a point (the sillier the better – but be careful with them. Keep them tasteful and make sure they won't offend – being offensive is not the wisest outstanding moment to create).
- A prop or object, again to illustrate a point, to provoke discussion or to give the audience something to stir their interest. (An object can be handed around the audience even before you've explained what it is or why it's significant for your message – an example of priming.)
- Video clips or particular pieces of music (again, be careful to make sure they won't offend).
- We've even seen an outstanding moment done as a single word written on a flip chart at the start of the presentation. The presenter writes the word up carefully and deliberately, turns to look at the audience, pauses (says nothing), waits...and then starts their presentation without telling us what the word's about. Now we're all waiting to find out, and paying attention until we do. This particular one is an example of an outstanding moment, the Zeigarnik Principle and priming.
- Anchoring. You can use any of the above to 'anchor' your messages – in this case we're thinking of an anchor as a strong association you create between a key message and one of the above examples. By showing your picture, prop or video clip a number of times (each time the key message is repeated), the idea is that at some point you'll only need to show people the picture, object or prop for them to recall the key message – and this might remain so in future.

Now, it's possible that you're cringing reading these, thinking that you've seen these kinds of things done too many times and they're kind of old hat and embarrassing. In our view the truth is the opposite: we haven't seen these things done many times at all; we can remember one or two – and they were good. In our view, people just aren't being brave enough with their outstanding moments. It takes guts to stop being a corporate robot, and most presentations we get to see which are happening week by week and day by day are just not memorable or even interesting.

If you use any of the above too much or too often, they *will* become embarrassing; if the rest of your presentation isn't good enough then using the ideas above *might* be embarrassing, but if you've got a good presentation and you deliver with confidence and credibility, these approaches will add to that confidence and credibility.

Finally, remember that too many outstanding moments will result in no outstanding moments – they'll begin to fight for attention, undermine each other, or just make the message one long outstanding moment (so nothing stands out anymore).

You don't need to create all the outstanding moments yourself. Pay attention to potential outstanding moments as they happen. These include:

- Interruptions from the audience.
- Interruptions from outside (someone walking into the room, or someone's phone ringing).

- Equipment failure, e.g. computer, projector, TV, DVD, teleconference etc.
- A question someone asks.
- A fire alarm.

And so on...the list is endless.

To make these moments useful, somehow you need to grab hold of them and bolt your seven to nine key ideas onto them. And to do this you have to be brave (if not confident). For example:

- Somebody's phone rings – wait for the tut-tuts of their colleagues to die down, then happily talk about the ringtone. Maybe it has a name, maybe you can sing it, maybe you can't but you ask if anybody else can, maybe you ask if somebody has something with more of a beat – and wait while they play it.
- Somebody arrives late – again, you wait for the tut-tuts of their colleagues to die down, then happily and confidently welcome the new person, ask them something about themselves, and tell them they haven't missed anything much yet. Then use this opportunity to summarise what you've covered so far again (making use of repetition, and new primacy and recency as a result of your Zeigarnik moment).

The Zeigarnik Principle

Don't worry about silence in your presentation – take your time, knowing that it'll help your audience process what they're hearing and seeing.

If you don't want to deal with interruptions by making them into outstanding moments as described above, you can be confident that they'll function just fine as straightforward interruptions. There's no need to be put off by an interruption of any kind – your job is just to pause and wait, confident that it's helping your presentation, and knowing that it's not a distraction, it's a way to make your presentation better.

Chapter Twelve

Tools and materials

Materials and tools are the things you bring to your presentation in order to convey your content. There's a long list of these to choose from. Here are a few examples:

Tools
Desks/tables
Projector
Microphone
Lectern
Flip chart
Pens
Presentation boards
Chairs

Materials
A4, A3, A2 or A1 paper (displaying your content)
Handouts
Reference documents
Books to read from
Slide deck (displaying your content)
Objects of interest relevant to your content
Music

Samples of product or ideas which are under discussion
Objects of interest of no relevance to your content, but which are part of your structure to change your state or the state of your audience
Videos and film clips
Audio clips and podcasts

All seems pretty obvious!

As you can see, the distinction between what constitutes 'materials' and what constitutes 'tools' is blurry. As we've said before, it doesn't really matter: whether you finally decide that film clips are tools or materials isn't actually relevant. What we've noticed is that if people don't consider their materials *and* their tools then they miss something – they forget to consider some important possibilities.

The selection of materials and tools should arise from your analysis of your audience, the development of your objectives and the conclusions you've drawn from these about your structure.

For example, if your objective is *to get people thinking differently*, then it stands to reason you might want to use different tools from the ones they're used to.

If you know your audience will have been sitting still all day looking at the same screen, give them a different experience, a different perspective – deliberately choose not to use a projector. Now you can consider what to do instead, and what materials and tools suggest themselves. You could use presentation boards, you could put your content onto a flip chart; you might even just put your content onto A3 paper.

Once you get your thinking this far, then you can consider how these tools and materials give you more flexibility about where to locate yourself. You could present at the opposite end of the room where there's no overhead projector, you could stick your A3 pages to the wall, you could arrange them down the middle of the table in front of your audience, or you could stand them on boards to the side of the table.

Notice again the kinds of mindset shifts and balances that you'll need to address in yourself in order to choose these kinds of options. Can you hear the whispering of your corporate robot? Can you hear it tempting you with the 'need' to be robotic?

That won't look credible	That won't look professional
I want to fit in	I don't want to be different

Of course you can; it's so easy for us all to do the same thing as everyone else all the time because we're afraid things just won't 'look right'.

These aren't trivial mindset choices though; it's going to be very important to 'fit in', to 'look professional' and to make sure you don't 'look too different'. As always, this is the significance of your audience analysis and your objective – you need to consider what you're trying to achieve and who you're talking to. You need to do this consciously and identify whether doing something different on this occasion will help convey your message. And you need to consider consciously whether there's anyone in the room who you can guess will reject your message solely on the grounds that your materials and tools 'don't look professional'. In the last eighteen years of delivering training and presenting to people we've had this experience twice – two decision-makers who couldn't embrace the message we were communicating. On both occasions they couldn't engage with our message properly because they didn't like the fact that we were presenting it on pieces of paper (coloured, laminated paper at that!). If we'd put a tiny bit more thought into our audience analysis on these two occasions, we could have predicted this response and done something to manage it better.

Just to be clear, this book is not called *Throw Away Your Projector*; there are plenty of presentations and meetings where all that's required to achieve your objective with the audience you have is to use a projector and to sit or stand in the same place as everyone else that day. What we *are* recommending is that you think about each presentation (just a little bit), and identify those moments where you need to kill the robot, and change your materials and tools, because:

I want to get my message across   I want to make an impact

I want them to wake up and engage

I want to be memorable

Of course, given an objective like getting people thinking differently, and given a situation in which you know your audience has been looking at the same screen all day, your decision about materials and tools might be to dispose of them altogether and just talk to the audience. Again, once you've got this far, then notice further opportunities to kill the robot – you don't need to stand in the place unconsciously allotted for presenting.

- You could sit instead.
- You could stay sitting exactly where you've sat all day, and have everyone turn to you.
- You could move to a different seat at the table.
- You could move about the room with purpose (or aimlessly) while you talk.

Now, when we listed example tools and materials at the start of this chapter, you might have thought it a little strange that we included desks/tables and chairs. Well, it's always worth considering the obvious. If we continue to assume the same objectives and audience analysis as above, then you might consider delivering your presentation in a space with no tables, or no chairs. This may sound weird but we've seen it done very effectively, e.g. breaking from the meeting room to go to the coffee shop together, or the coffee machine, or just out into the corridor and delivering your session there.

These choices should be purposeful, rather than just random weirdness; it will help if your audience can recognise that they've been sitting in the same position too long and that a move to a different part of the room, or out of the room altogether, will be helpful. Equally, don't be too careful – most people don't ever consider doing these kinds of things, which, once again, is why so many of us end up sitting in boring meetings over and over again where every message is very similar if not exactly the same, and it's very difficult to stay awake and interested through the day.

A few more examples of how we've used materials or tools in presentations we've made, in order to achieve very specific things with audience and structure:

- Four flip charts – one in each corner of the room, each displaying one part of the structure of the presentation (e.g. background, objective, methods or measurement). We walked from one to the other as we presented, and the audience, seated in the middle, turned to look in different directions. They loved it and thought it incredibly different, even though in every other respect it was a very conventional presentation.
- Once we went to a presentation with a pile of pink and blue pieces of A4 paper. (We had a printed presentation on white A4 paper as well, but we kept that in our bags, under the table.) As we talked with the audience, we wrote on the pieces of paper in front of them every time we heard the key mindset moves that were required in the organisation, and we placed them in columns on the table – pink to the left, blue to the right. After about five minutes the most senior member of the audience stopped us and laughed.

"I love you folks," he said. "I've been sitting here all day, listening to the same old, same old. And everybody who's presented leaves me with a print-off of their deck of slides to read." (Here he pointed at a stack of white paper, several centimetres thick, on the corner of the table, and as he pointed, he groaned.) "Instead, you folks make me think, and you get your message into my head straight away, in a manner that I'll remember – and best of all, you don't leave me with more work to do afterwards." Quietly, we reached under the table to zip up our bags, just in case our A4 printed presentation tried to escape onto the table at the end of our presentation.

- Short readings which illustrate key messages, printed onto A5 cards and handed out to random audience members for them to read at various points during the presentation. Be careful with this one – make sure you don't spring a nasty surprise on someone with a reading or learning difficulty.

- Consider how to introduce more colour into presentations (again, as a way to wake up the audience, and provide a contrast from the standard colour scheme in use, which is often in line with the organisation's brand). Introduce a distinctly contrasting colour of text box, or change the colour of font on particular words or ideas to signify different things, e.g. actions or recommendations in a particular colour, barriers in another colour. When we do this, we don't necessarily point it out – people quickly pick it up anyway. *Don't use too much colour or too many different fonts – you could induce cognitive strain.*

Different colours and fonts will require more brain power from your audience – too much of it may encourage them into a trance because they're already too tired, and they can't cope with such a demand for cognitive functioning.

- Objects which illustrate your message or complement your message – you can place these on the table at the beginning or hand them around for examination. A key decision is whether to highlight the object in question or not. Often by highlighting it you make the association too clumsy or cringeworthy – like a joke that stops being funny when you have to explain it. We've seen it done well where an object, a picture or a word is displayed at the beginning of a presentation, and not explained until the end. Equally we've seen it done well where an object, a picture or a word was displayed all the way through a presentation and never explained. When the presenter left the room audience members discussed why it had been displayed, offering their own interpretations and thereby prolonging consideration of the key messages of the presentation.

- Of course, the same kind of impact can be achieved just by making sure that you bring a 'product sample'. For example, if you're presenting about a new process or service which is being developed, find a way to make it physical with an object or pictures that demonstrate it. These don't need to be displayed in a linear fashion – you can display them all on the wall away from your presentation, and have people refer to them throughout your message. (As we've said before, if you're not feeling so confident then this can be a helpful approach to move the spotlight and attention away from you.)

Finally, the crucial point about materials – check your mindsets. Are your materials there to:

Illustrate or add interest to my content

Increase the impact or power of my content

Make my content more memorable

Or are they there to:

Deliver your words for you

Repeat your words

Let your audience read your words while you speak them

On this occasion we totally disagree with the pink mindsets. All too often we see presenters use their materials only to *deliver* or *repeat* their words for them. The most obvious example of this is when the presenter uses a sequence of projector slides on which they display the sentences they're speaking – sometimes exactly the same.

It is our view that if you end up with this scenario you haven't identified why you're bothering with a presentation at all – you might as well send an email instead, or type up your content on a piece of A4 paper and pass it round for people to read, then respond to questions at the end; or do the same with the overhead projector, but just stay sitting silently in your seat while the audience reads through your slides (strangely enough, this might actually be different enough to make a refreshing and impactful change in the meeting).

Consider how you might use your materials to summarise, illustrate or make your five to nine key points more memorable, e.g.:

- Summarise some (or all) of your key points with a picture (but make it an interesting or memorable picture we're unlikely to have seen before).
- Summarise each of your key points with one word.
- Summarise some of your key points with an object instead.
- Use a graph or simple piece of data to summarise one of your key points.

And so on...

Finally, if you're going to use your materials differently, the essential ingredient is confidence: whatever you decide to do, you have to be able to do it with confidence or at least fake your confidence well enough. If you apologise for your use of tools and materials, or if you somehow don't stand up for your choices when challenged, then they won't work for you – they'll work against you.

Chapter Thirteen

Content

There's not much to say about content. By the time you've worked on other elements of MASCOT™, content should start to suggest itself.

There are a number of issues on which to challenge yourself. We've covered them already elsewhere, but here they are again:

I must fill the time I've got

vs. I need time to repeat key messages

or I need less content than the time available

I can't run out of steam – I'll look stupid

vs. Less really can be more

or Extra content could increase analysis

I must cover all the detail

vs. Relevant information is all that's needed

or Present simplicity (but have the detail available when asked)

Know your content. Know your argument, but don't attempt to remember every detail about it – you can prepare handouts and visual aids for this.

Prepare the detail you'll need in order to answer all kinds of questions, but don't present it unless you're asked, or until the response you're getting suggests it's needed. (Keep it, literally, under the table and reveal it only when it becomes necessary.)

Don't put together enough content to fill the time available – be prepared to finish early.

Simplify, and then simplify again – rewrite once or twice, with the sole aim of reducing the amount of information by half each time. Know that you might need help with this one, from someone who cares about the content less than you.

Be aware that adding more content and more detail will sometimes encourage your audience to become more thoughtful, more analytical and want more detail about specific parts of your presentation, which may hamper your ability to get through the whole of your message on time.

Keep the language and the content itself simple and easy to understand. Complexity of language again risks encouraging your audience into complexity of thinking, which may hamper your ability to get through.

Use your visual aids to prompt or illustrate your content – don't load them down with the content itself. Think of the visual aids as providing the footsteps and milestones of your story – you'll speak your content to fill in around these footsteps, milestones and illustrations.

Chapter Fourteen

You are your primary presentation tool – so get yourself ready

Back in Chapter 8 we described the two steps involved in preparing for a presentation: the planning step and the pre-check step.

Most of this book has been about the planning step. This step is about planning '*it*' – the presentation: the message, materials, audience, structure, content, objectives and tools you're going to use. Remember, the pre-check step is different – it's about '*me*'; getting '*me*' ready. This is crucial. Since you are the primary tool you'll be using to communicate your message, you should do something deliberate to get 'you' ready.

Here's an example. A couple of days before writing this we were observing a board meeting. At two o'clock in the afternoon, after four and a half hours of agenda items, it was the turn of the Finance Director to give a quick update. It appeared to us that he'd done his planning – he'd prepared about ten minutes of information, he'd chosen to present it sitting in his chair with no visual aids, he had only three or four points to make, and he knew the state his audience might be in, so he intended to keep it informal, light and quick.

He launched in: he spoke quickly and eloquently without pause and in one continuous, constant rhythm. No variation in tone, no variation in speed, and taking very few breaths. He was eloquent, provocative and used a smattering of long, intellectual words. At one point some way in he made an aside – an instruction that if people wanted more information they should talk to another member of the team sitting nearby – and he did this without a pause for breath, and without a pause in what he was saying, so that it was barely noticeable that this instructional aside was not part of the thing he was talking about at the time.

The content was good, the structure was good (enough), but the amount of material was too much – enough for twenty minutes. The delivery, whilst startling, brilliantly articulate and witty, was inappropriate for the time of day or the amount of material, and was completely ineffective in getting the key points of his message across with clarity, impact and memorability.

Early on in his monologue, the HR director, sitting next to him, yawned; the operations director opposite him stretched, and the head of the sales director fell forwards slightly before jerking upright again – visibly avoiding a quick nap.

If the FD had wanted to induce a trance, or hypnotise the board, this performance was highly suitable. We felt we'd been squashed flat by a very clever steamroller, and had very little idea of what his three or four key points had been.

This kind of thing – where the performance of the presenter is inappropriate for the presentation that they've put together – is a common occurrence. It's entirely natural when the presenter is overwhelmingly focused on their presentation content, structure, tools or materials.

In the moments before the FD was asked to deliver his session he hadn't been preparing *himself*. We don't know what he was doing, but if he was preparing at all, we suspect that he was thinking about his content and his structure again (even though this was already planned). As we've said, it's possible he'd considered his audience, and the state they'd be in, but he hadn't considered himself, and prepared himself so that he would speak and communicate in a way that enabled his message to land. As a result, he'd delivered in a high-speed version of his usual communication style – and it didn't work.

Many of us expect to be able to communicate in a particular manner without preparing ourselves to do so. And many of us expect to be able to manage our typical habits of communication and change them without preparing ourselves to do so. Under pressure, both of these things become more difficult, not less. Under pressure it's quite possible that *you* will get in the way of your message; that you will get in the way of your beautifully crafted presentation. And that's because you haven't prepared yourself.

So, the pre-check is about getting *yourself* ready. This is about:

- Your objective (again).
- Your mindsets – how these will help or hinder you, and what might be better ones to adopt so you're in a good state to communicate.
- The behaviours you need to use (to suit your audience, to suit their state, and to enable the clear, impactful and interesting communication of your messages).
- The time you have – when you intend to finish your presentation, and this should loop straight back into your behaviours; the behaviours you'll need in order to get this done, and still keep your message clear, impactful and interesting.

Let's have a look at each of these:

Your Objective

Remind yourself of what you're really trying to do with this presentation (and what you're not) – focus on this rather than on all the content that you've planned.

Your Mindsets

Notice the state you're in and the messages you're giving yourself that might not be helpful to drive the state in you and the behaviours that you'll need (e.g. the FD seemed to have a mindset that there wasn't enough time and therefore he had to rush, rather than deciding that he didn't have enough time, and therefore he needed to slow down, calm down and pick his most important points).

The Behaviours To Use

(To suit your audience, to suit their state, and to enable the clear, impactful and interesting communication of your message).

This breaks down into two areas:

1. What you need to manage about your typical way of communicating (which might be inappropriate here).
2. What you want to be like/what you need to be like while you're communicating.

What you need to manage about your typical way of communicating (which might be inappropriate here).

- Consider the *behaviours* you know you're in danger of using when you're nervous, e.g. you know you speak faster and faster, without pausing and without breathing, or you know you start apologising for things you say, you know you go into too much detail, you know you get too loud and boisterous, or become too monotone.
- Consider the behaviours you know you're in danger of using when you're too comfortable or confident (when you start to show off), e.g. you know you start being too clever, you know you use unnecessarily long words or complex language, you know you get distracted and go off at tangents, or use unprofessional language or tell unprofessional stories or jokes.

What you want to be like/what you need to be like while you're communicating.

- Consider the *behaviours* you want to use while communicating, e.g. speed and variation of your speech in order to make sure people cope with your message.
- Consider the variation in behaviours you want to use. We sometimes think of this as Changing Gears®, e.g. as a minimum, thinking about the number of gears you might want to use, so that you don't get fixed in one relentless way of talking.
- Consider specific *behaviours* which will be important given the audience you're presenting to, e.g. the need to pause and smile sometimes, the need to hold the silence after particular points, or the need to hold your confidence and not jump into rushed responses to questions or challenges from the audience.

Of course the consideration of point 1 (what you need to manage about your typical way of communicating) needs to lead into point 2 (what you want to be like/what you need to be like). When you're ready to present, it's useful to be focused on what you want to be like, rather than what you want to avoid, so this sequencing of one into the other is vital.

The Time You Have

As you'll have read above, the conscious consideration of your time limit is vital – if you don't consider it properly and positively it will drive unhelpful behaviours in you (rushing, gabbling and nervousness), but if you do consider it properly you will be able to choose more powerful behaviours (be considered, be deliberate, pick your statements carefully and say little – less than planned, in order to get through in time and with clarity).

The key to the pre-check is to make sure it happens – make sure you don't think you're getting yourself ready, when all you're really doing is running back through your presentation (your structure and content) in your head. We see people doing this all the time – you need to know that it's too late now, and if you carry on you'll make yourself more nervous. Now's the time to focus on you and sort yourself out.

The other key to the pre-check is not to overdo it. If you do it for too long, once again, you'll work yourself into a nervous state, or you'll drive yourself into a reflective, analytical state, which may be entirely the wrong state for your audience or for getting your message across.

That's Enough For Now

We're in danger of getting beyond our five to nine chunks. Just remember, this is all about changing your mindset – moving beyond your assumptions about how to present with impact.

Let MASCOT™ guide your thinking:

> *Objective*: check why you're bothering to present.
> *Audience*: make an educated guess about how they'll respond, and...
> *Structure*: ...put across your message in a way designed to deal with this.
> Then pick the *Materials*, the *Tools* and the *Content* you need.

Remember, content is the wrong place to begin.

Know that interruptions, silences, mistakes, equipment failure and strange, unexpected occurrences will happen, but that if you deal with them appropriately and confidently, they can help your communication.

Don't try to cover too much (not enough to fill the time available); keep things simple, be confident that you can take your time, and pause – it will help your message and your audience.

Robot programmes are available, but you don't have to follow them – you are allowed to use tools, materials and formats in different ways. You don't have to begin and end with the usual formula; do something different – this will add to your impact.

Create some outstanding moments – have some fun!

Don't only plan your presentation – you're the primary tool, so pre-check yourself as well.

Every presentation is a significant communication opportunity, but this doesn't mean you have to treat it like a significant presentation. Do what's needed on each occasion. This means that on many occasions you should *embrace your robot, follow the formula and do exactly what everyone's expecting*, because that's what'll deliver your objective this time, for this particular audience, in an appropriate manner for the time and place.

But on other occasions, don't. You know what to do instead…

Kill the robot!

Find out more about Coloured Square at
www.colouredsquare.com

Lightning Source UK Ltd.
Milton Keynes UK
UKOW06f0610060417
298470UK00010B/46/P